SHIRE NATUR

TH GREY SEAL

SHEILA ANDERSON

CONTENTS
Introduction 2
How to identify Grey Seals 4
Distribution and numbers 6
Feeding 11
Reproduction 15
Life and death 18
Grey Seals and man 19
How and where to see Grey Seals 23
Further reading 24

COVER: *Two female Grey Seals coming ashore at the Farne Islands.*

Series editors: Jim Flegg and Chris Humphries

Copyright © 1988 by Sheila Anderson. First published 1988.
Number 26 in the Shire Natural History series. ISBN 0 85263 947 3.
All rights reserved. No part of this publication may be reproduced or transmitted in any form or by any means, electronic or mechanical, including photocopy, recording, or any information storage and retrieval system, without permission in writing from the publishers, Shire Publications Ltd, Cromwell House, Church Street, Princes Risborough, Aylesbury, Bucks HP17 9AJ, UK.

Set in 9 point Times roman and printed in Great Britain by C. I. Thomas & Sons (Haverfordwest) Ltd, Press Buildings, Merlins Bridge, Haverfordwest, Dyfed.

Introduction

The Grey Seal *(Halichoerus grypus)* is one of two species of seal which breed around the shores of Britain. It is strongly associated with the British Isles because almost half of the world population of 200,000 occurs in British waters. Its distribution is limited to the north Atlantic and the Baltic, in contrast to that of the other British breeding species, the Common Seal *(Phoca vitulina)*, which is found throughout the northern hemisphere and has a total population in the region of 500,000. The British population is estimated to be at least 25,000. Britain receives occasional visits from other species of seal, vagrants from the north such as Walrus, Harp, Hooded, Bearded and Ringed seals, but none of these breeds in British waters.

Seals are mammals and are related to the carnivores, the sharp-toothed meat eaters. They are part of a group known as the Pinnipedia (the 'flap-footed' animals), which includes the true seals, sealions, fur seals and the Walrus. Their origins lie in the terrestrial carnivores of about 25 million years ago, though their exact ancestry is shrouded in mystery because the fossil record of the early pinnipeds is extremely sparse. The sealions, fur seals and the Walrus (collectively known as the Otaroidea) are thought to have evolved around the shores of the Pacific basin from a bear-like ancestor, while the true seals (the Phocoidea) arose slightly later from an otter-like ancestor in what is now the north Atlantic region. Whether or not they have separate ancestry, the pinnipeds share a number of features — they are all superbly adapted to life in the water.

AQUATIC ADAPTATIONS

For a warm-blooded mammal with a body temperature around 37 C (99 F) water is a cold place. Even in tropical areas the sea temperature is usually lower than 37 C, and in polar waters it is often near freezing. Seals keep warm by insulating themselves with a thick layer of subcutaneous fat, known as blubber. In addition they have an outer covering of hair which helps to keep out the cold, particularly in the aptly named fur seals, which have very dense fur coats. The blubber layer also helps to pad their outline, smoothing and streamlining their shape to aid in fast swimming. The standard mammalian limbs are modified into stiff or webbed paddles to propel the seal through the water. These modifications are chiefly shortening of the limb bones which leave the 'hands' and 'feet' protruding from the body as manoeuvrable flippers. The otarid seals and the Walrus swim by sculling themselves along using their well developed fore-flippers, but phocid seals use strong sideways movements of the hind flippers as the main propulsive force.

Mammals have to breathe air, and seals are no exception. How are they able to spend a large proportion of their time under water? Seals are able to take large reserves of oxygen down with them and when they do come up to breathe they can exchange gases very quickly. The oxygen stores are not in the form of gas, which would make diving difficult and would lead to the problem of 'bends' on re-surfacing, but are combined with pigments, such as haemoglobin, which have a strong affinity for oxygen. In relation to their body size, seals have a huge volume of blood, which contains large quantities of haemoglobin, but they also have oxygen-carrying pigments in their muscles, known as myoglobin, so the working tissues carry a store of vital oxygen. Seals can carry about three times as much oxygen in their bodies as land mammals of a comparable size. Another key factor enabling them to spend a very short time at the surface is their ability to get rid of carbon dioxide and take in oxygen with remarkable speed. So, for short dives they rely on their copious stores of oxygen and make frequent but very short visits to the surface. For longer dives more drastic changes to their physiology are needed to help them conserve oxygen. They reduce their heart rate to only a few beats per minute and restrict blood circulation to just the essential organs for the duration of the dive, which in Elephant and Weddell seals can be for as long as an hour.

Another seal characteristic associated

with life in the water is the tendency to large body size. As size increases, the surface area over which heat can be lost does not increase at the same rate as volume increases. Keeping warm is thus favoured by large size. Furthermore, large animals can swim faster than smaller ones. The smallest seal, the Ringed Seal, weighs about 65 kg (143 pounds), which is big compared to most land mammals, but tiny compared to the Southern Elephant Seal, which can weigh as much as 4 tonnes.

BACK TO THE LAND

In spite of these splendid adaptations to life on and under the sea, there is one aspect of seals' life history which gives away their terrestrial ancestry. Unlike whales, the pinnipeds are not totally aquatic animals: they still return to land to give birth to their young. But their physical adaptations to an aquatic existence make them clumsy on land compared with their grace and agility when swimming. On land therefore they are vulnerable to terrestrial predators. Breeding sites tend to be remote, inaccessible places such as offshore islands or floating ice. Pups are relatively helpless when born and are not ready to take to the sea, except Common Seal pups, which are born between the tides and have to be able to swim within six hours or less. Like all young mammals, seal pups are fed on milk during the land-based lactation period. In phocid seals this time can be very short — as little as four days in Hooded Seals. The end of lactation marks the end of maternal care and the end of the time when seals are relatively easy to study. Once at sea, they are hard to observe, although advances in electronic telemetry equipment are allowing researchers to track them.

Not long ago the breeding season of seals was not the time that man studied them but the time he could most easily kill them. Their aquatic adaptations enhanced their attractions as a prey species: large size, fur coat and blubber which could be rendered down to oil. Now there is less demand for seal products and a greater awareness of scientific conservation issues. Today's concerns are less with the problems of commercial over-exploitation of seal stocks but are focused on the interactions between marine mammals and fisheries.

1. *Close-up of a female Grey Seal.*

How to identify Grey Seals

A whiskery face, head up, peering out of the sea is not likely to be anything other than a seal, though in some coastal areas there might be a chance of seeing an Otter *(Lutra lutra)*. But the much smaller, flatter head of the Otter, with its broad muzzle, is quite distinctive. If the Otter sees you, it will disappear quickly, whereas a seal will be likely to have at least one more quizzical look. But which seal is it? At a casual glance Grey and Common Seal look quite similar, particularly if the view is of a head sinking beneath the waves. The characteristics to concentrate on to tell them apart are size, head shape and coat colour.

Grey Seals are large mammals, indeed the largest of British mammals (if the whales are excluded). The shape is an elongated torpedo, typical of phocid seals. The fore-flipper is paddle-shaped and bears long slender claws in young animals, but these may be worn and short in older animals. The hind flippers are fan-shaped and faintly concave when stretched, as the outer digits are slightly longer than the central three. The digits are joined by a hair-covered web. The males are bigger than the females. They are about 2 metres (6 feet 6 inches) long when mature, compared with 1.8 metres (6 feet) for females, but the males are half as heavy again — about 230 kg (4½ cwt) compared to the females at 150 kg (3 cwt). When seen on land, the heavy neck and shoulders of a male are very obvious if it is next to the more slightly built female. Common Seals are much smaller beasts, and the males are only slightly larger than the females. An average weight for a Common Seal would be 80-100 kg (1½ to 2 cwt). But size is a difficult characteristic to assess, particularly if the animal is on its own or if seven-eighths of it are under the water. A better way of telling the two British breeding species apart is by looking at the heads. Grey Seals have an elongated muzzle whereas Common Seals look quite snub-nosed. The snout of male Grey Seals is convex in profile, giving a 'Roman' nose, but the female's is much flatter. The nostrils when closed appear as parallel slits in Grey Seals whereas

2. *Grey and Common Seal head shapes. Note the elongated muzzle of the Grey Seal (above) and how the nostrils appear almost parallel when viewed head-on.*

3. Male (left) and female Grey Seals exchanging threats on a breeding beach. Note the differences in size, head shape and coat colouration.

4. Male (left), female and white-coated pup in the dunes on Sable Island, Nova Scotia, Canada.

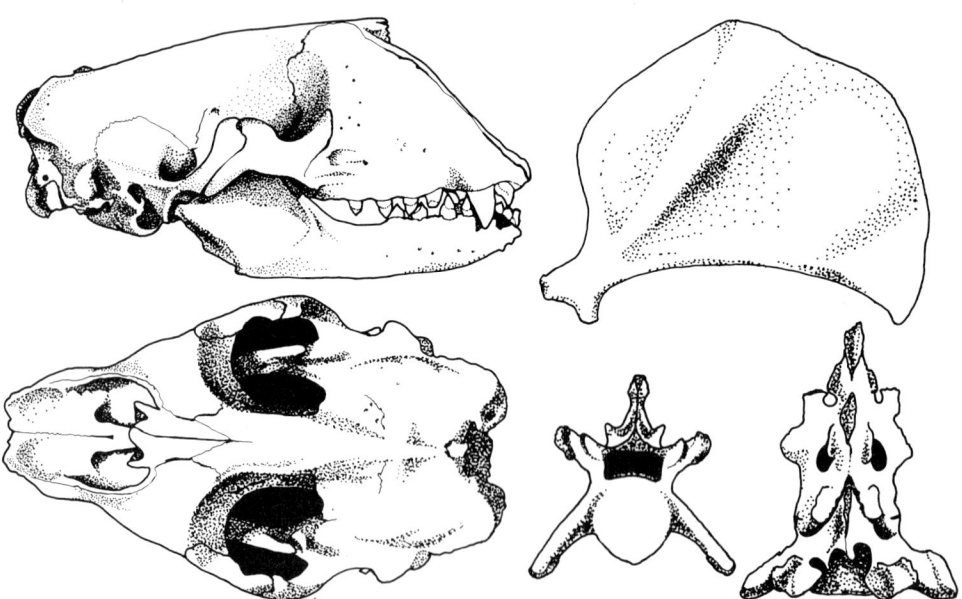

5. *Some easily recognised bones of Grey Seals: (top and bottom left) skull viewed from side and from above; (top right) scapula; (bottom centre) vertebra; (bottom right) sacrum.*

those of the Common Seal almost meet at the base, forming a V shape.

Common Seals tend to have an all-over spotted pelage, but Grey Seal coat colouration is very variable. The markings of both species are generally more obvious when the fur is wet. Grey Seal males tend to be uniformly dark grey or brown with a few pale patches; the belly is slightly lighter than the back. Females are usually medium grey on the back, shading to pale grey or cream on the belly, with dark patches sparsely scattered on the lighter background. Enormous variation occurs in colouring and patterning of Grey Seal females, from very pale uniform colour with almost no spots to dark females whose patches nearly coalesce. All shades of light and dark grey, brown and silver occur. A few adults of both sexes may be completely black and some individuals may have ginger colouration, particularly on the head. Just before the moult, when the hair is worn, the general colouration is brown or fawn, especially when the pelage dries. Females moult between January and March, males from March to May. Pups are born in white fluffy fur which is shed in two to three weeks, revealing the first adult coat.

Most people would prefer to see a live seal than to study the remains of a dead one, although the opportunities to examine a corpse are limited as it is quite rare for dead seals to be washed up. Regular beachcombers, particularly of Grey Seal breeding beaches, may come across the occasional one which dies on or near the shore. The best finds are bleached bones on the strand line (whole seals can be difficult to deal with and very smelly).

Distribution and numbers

It is thought that Grey Seals were once found throughout the north Atlantic region but that the advance of ice during the last glaciation about twenty thousand years ago separated them into eastern and western stocks. The Baltic Grey Seals would have been cut off from the rest of the eastern stock when the forerunner of the Baltic Sea, the Ancylus Lake, was formed about nine thousand years ago. There are therefore now three populations, one in the west Atlantic, one in the east Atlantic and one in the Baltic, between which there is no interchange of individuals. In the west, Grey Seals breed on the ice in the Gulf of St Lawrence and on the islands off Nova Scotia, the most important of which is Sable Island. They are found on the coast of North America from Hebron, Labrador, in the north to Nantucket, Massachusetts, in the south. On the other side of the Atlantic, they breed around Iceland, the Faroes, the coast of Norway from More northwards to the North Cape, and on the Murman coast of the USSR, but the largest numbers are found around the coast of the British Isles. The Outer Hebrides and the Orkney Islands are the main breeding centres. Small uninhabited islands are favoured, such as Gasker, Shillay, North Rona and the Monach Isles in the Hebridean group and the Greenholms, Holm of Faray and Auskerry in Orkney. On the east coast of Britain, small numbers are found on the coasts of Norfolk and Lincolnshire, and larger numbers at the Farne Islands, Isle of May and Shetland Islands. The southwestern coasts of Ireland, Wales and England have scattered groups of Grey Seals which occur on small beaches and in caves. The Baltic population is the smallest of the three, with Grey Seals being found mainly in the Gulfs of Bothnia, Riga and Finland. There are estimated to be 2000 Grey Seals in the Baltic and between 71,000 and 125,000 in the west Atlantic. The east Atlantic stock is estimated to be 113,500 (Iceland 10,000, Faroes 3000, Great Britain 92,000, Ireland 2000, Norway 3500, USSR 3000).

The favoured haunts of breeding Grey Seals in Britain are exposed rocky coasts, islands and caves, but they are found at other times in most coastal habitats. The largest assemblies occur on uninhabited islands, where seals may spread over the entire top of the island, such as on Gasker in the Outer Hebrides. They have even taken to climbing hills in search of a suitable place: on North Rona a few seals ascend a steep hill 80 metres (260 feet) high to pup on a grassy ridge overlooking the main breeding area. Smaller groups are found in sheltered coves and on fringing beaches of islands or at a few sites on the mainland where steep cliffs prevent people from gaining access. Sea caves are used for pupping, particularly in the south-west of Wales and England, but an important criterion is the existence of a secure beach at the back of the cave above the reach of the tides. Pups are born on sandbanks or sandy beaches at only a few locations, such as Donna Nook in Lincolnshire and the Monach Isles in the Outer Hebrides.

Outside the breeding season we know much less about the distribution of the species. Animals are still found around the breeding sites, but they rarely use the same islands or beaches that are occupied

6. *The numbers and distribution of Grey Seals in Britain.*

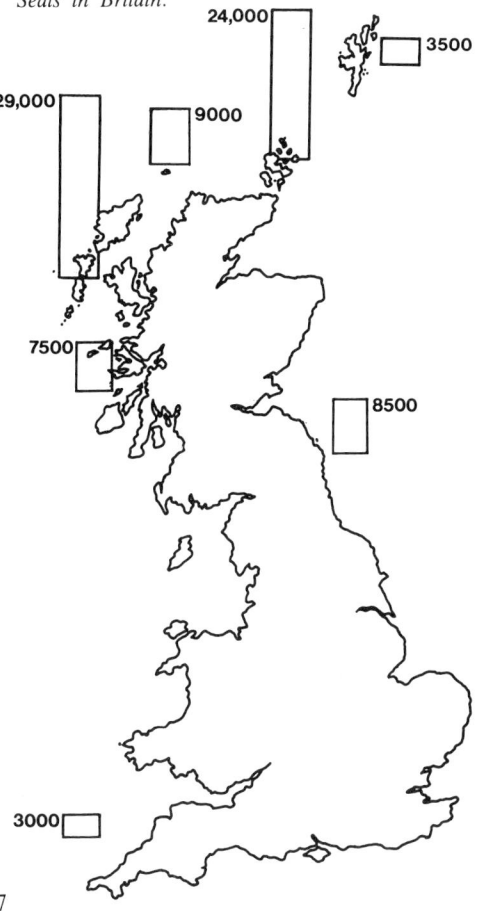

7. Grey Seal pup on pack ice in the Gulf of St Lawrence, Canada.

8. Densely packed breeding Grey Seals at the Farne Islands, Northumberland.

9. *A Grey Seal male eating a large salmon.*

10. *A newborn pup, blood-stained from its recent birth, receiving the first feed of fat-rich milk.*

for breeding. Although some large groups do occur, particularly at the time of the moult in early spring when they shed their hair and grow a new coat, in general the numbers seen are a small fraction of those known to breed at the site. So where are they? They are probably at sea feeding, but exactly where is more difficult to specify. However, enormous advances are now being made in discovering their whereabouts and patterns of behaviour through the use of radio telemetry. Small electronic packages sealed in watertight, pressure-resistant cases are glued to the fur. The most commonly used devices are VHF radio transmitters which can only be heard when the seal is at the surface or hauled out on land. The signals can be picked up either on a portable receiver with a hand-held aerial or on an automatic recording station with an aerial in a fixed place. These are useful for recording the pattern of hauling-out behaviour. The range is, however, limited to about 10-15 km (6-9 miles), so if the seal goes out of range of the receiver the signal will not be heard. More sophisticated devices, which use UHF radio transmission, beam a signal up to an orbiting satellite, which enables a seal to be tracked miles from any receiving station based on land or boat.

Some fascinating glimpses of the free-swimming behaviour of Grey Seals have been obtained by using a combination of VHF and underwater sonic devices on the same animal. One seal was tracked continuously for nine days from a boat fitted with hydrophones and receivers. During this time it went from the Farne Islands in Northumberland up to Dundee, stopping at the Isle of May and the Firth of Forth. When travelling, it maintained a speed of about 4.5 km (2¾ miles) per hour and moved in remarkably straight lines, indicating a strong navigational sense. The equipment included a depth sensor, so the dive depth was recorded. Two dive patterns were noted: one was a 'spike' shaped dive which occurred when the seal was travelling and the other was a 'square' shaped dive which was interpreted as a feeding dive,

11. *Gluing a VHF radio transmitter to the fur of a female.*

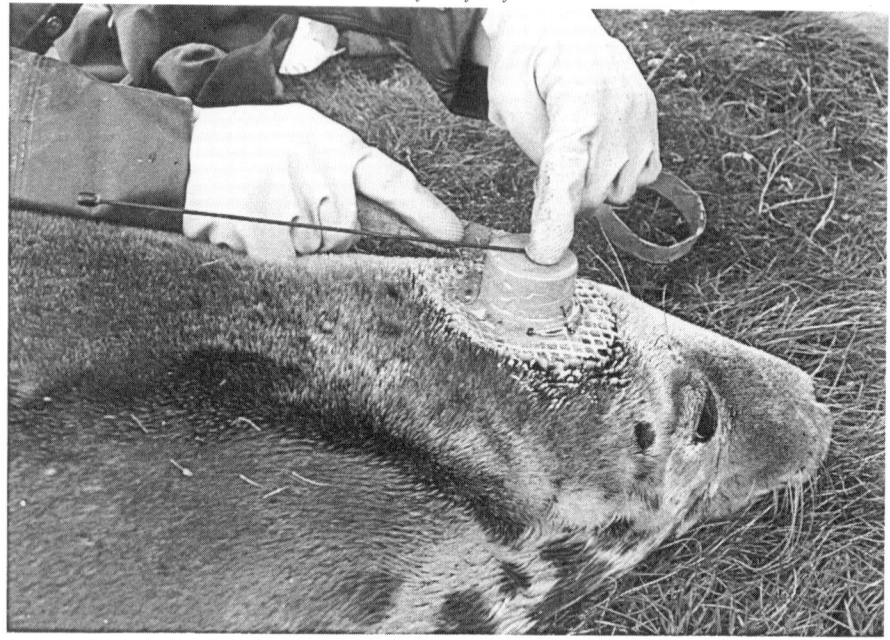

during which the seal foraged at or near the sea bed. Some of the latest devices being developed incorporate swimming speed sensors, heart rate recorders and mini-computers/data loggers which collate and synthesise biological information over a period of time and then transmit it to a receiver when required to do so. It should be possible to build up a picture of the range that seals may cover and the areas of the seas which are favoured for feeding. Such information is critical to an understanding of the interactions between seals and fisheries.

Feeding

A newly weaned Grey Seal pup, abandoned by its mother at the end of lactation, has to find its own way into the sea and learn which of the things around it are edible. Mistakes are made: pups have been found with grass, seaweed and stones in their stomachs. Better choices are shrimps and crabs, which often feature in the diet of young seals. But all seals soon move on to their main prey, fish. What are their favourite species? Early studies of diet were based on stomach contents of dead seals, a large sample of which were taken at salmon fishing nets. The results of these investigations suggested, not surprisingly, that salmon featured prominently on the seals' menu. More recent work has used faecal samples, from which the hard parts of food items, which have survived digestion, can be sieved. The advantages of using these are that no seals are killed in the study and a vast number of samples can be gathered throughout the year from a variety of sites where seals haul out. The disadvantages (besides having to sieve vast quantities of material) are largely those of interpreting the material collected. The fish remains which are particularly important in identifying the species are the ear stones or otoliths. The smallest of these might be partially or even totally dissolved by the seal's digestive juices. Seals may not always eat the head of the fish, particularly if it is a large specimen, so what comes out may not necessarily reflect exactly what went in.

Nonetheless, faecal analysis is still the best available method of determining the composition of Grey Seal diet. Laboratory experiments which involve feeding known food items to captive seals are helping to interpret the hard remains of fish from faeces and are also exploring whether proteins from different fish species can be identified from the soft faecal material.

These studies reveal that Grey Seals eat whatever species are abundant in the area which they frequent. Although many of the same species occur in samples from all around the coast, the proportions of them vary between samples from different places. Comparisons with the composition of the catch in the commercial fisheries around the British coast indicate that the diet of seals in a particular area coincides roughly with what is available. Two surprising aspects of the results are the importance of sand-eels in the diet in many areas and the complete absence of salmon remains, although it is known that seals do eat some salmon. Sand-eels are small fish, not taken for human consumption, but commercially important as a component of fishmeal, and extremely important in the diet of other marine predators such as seabirds. The absence of salmon from Grey Seal faecal samples could be because seals do not eat the heads of these large fish, so the otoliths do not appear in the samples, but it is still odd that even the distinctive scales are not found, particularly as it is known from the laboratory studies that seals which have been fed with salmon do have scales in their faeces. Although fish are the major prey of Grey Seals, other marine creatures such as squid, shrimps, crabs and other crustaceans are occasionally taken. Grey Seals have even been known to take seabirds swimming at the surface.

How they capture fish seems straightforward — a quick burst of speed, a forward thrust of the neck and a snap of the jaws. Small fish under a kilogram will go down in one gulp, but larger fish are held in the fore-flippers while chunks are torn off by the teeth. Claw marks found on the flanks of a salmon may be the sign of a fish that escaped a seal's grasp. Some fish, such as lumpsuckers, are skinned

12. *A pup aged two to three days.*

13. *A fat white-coated pup, twelve to fifteen days old.*

14. *A weaned pup with most of its white fur moulted.*

15. *A pup four weeks old, fully moulted and ready for independent life.*

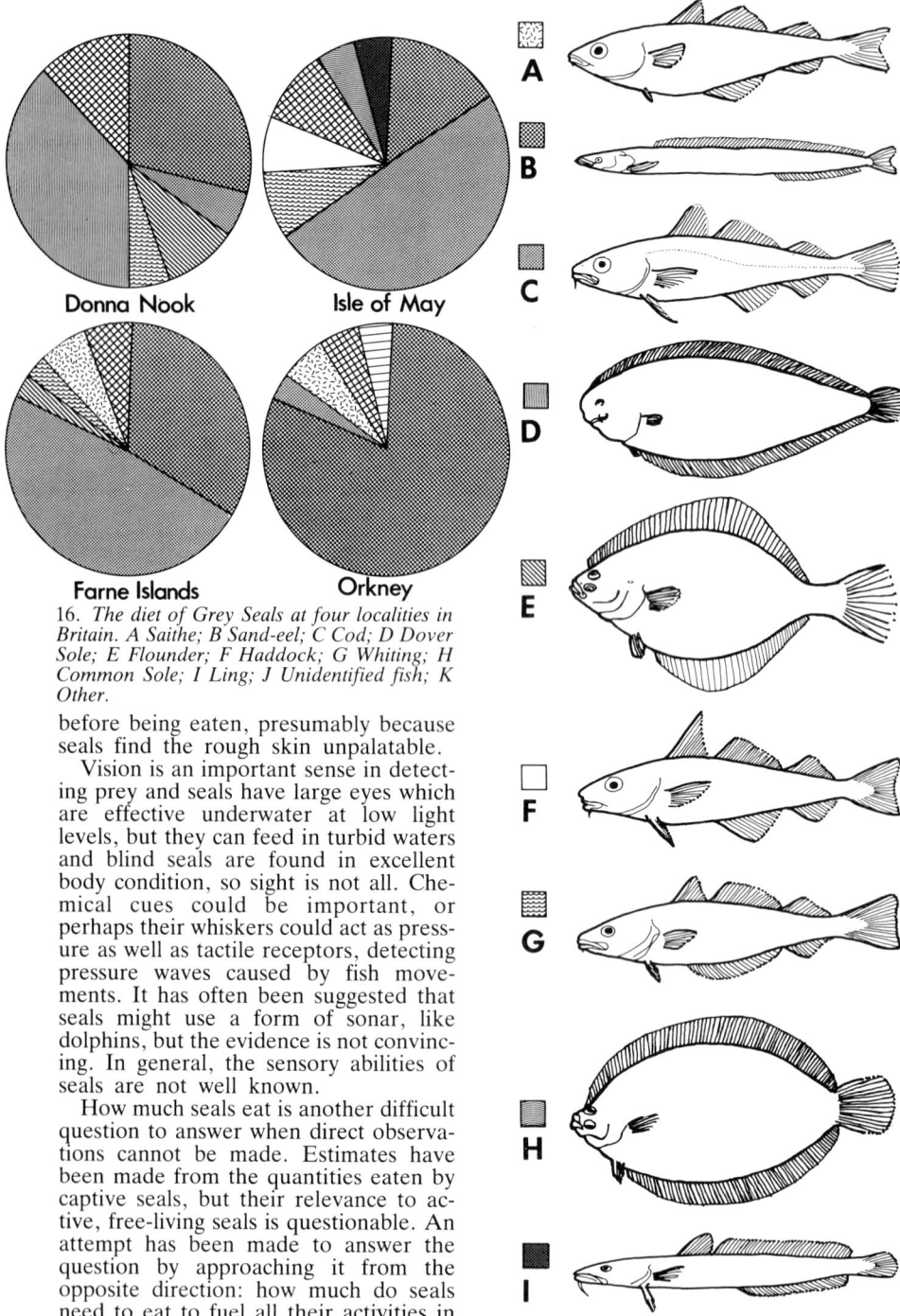

16. *The diet of Grey Seals at four localities in Britain. A Saithe; B Sand-eel; C Cod; D Dover Sole; E Flounder; F Haddock; G Whiting; H Common Sole; I Ling; J Unidentified fish; K Other.*

before being eaten, presumably because seals find the rough skin unpalatable.

Vision is an important sense in detecting prey and seals have large eyes which are effective underwater at low light levels, but they can feed in turbid waters and blind seals are found in excellent body condition, so sight is not all. Chemical cues could be important, or perhaps their whiskers could act as pressure as well as tactile receptors, detecting pressure waves caused by fish movements. It has often been suggested that seals might use a form of sonar, like dolphins, but the evidence is not convincing. In general, the sensory abilities of seals are not well known.

How much seals eat is another difficult question to answer when direct observations cannot be made. Estimates have been made from the quantities eaten by captive seals, but their relevance to active, free-living seals is questionable. An attempt has been made to answer the question by approaching it from the opposite direction: how much do seals need to eat to fuel all their activities in the annual cycle? The energy costs of lactation, breeding, swimming, diving, fighting and so on can be measured. The energy requirements can then be converted into how much fish has to be eaten to meet these needs. The quantity will vary depending on the species favoured in the diet; for instance, a seal which favoured energy-rich species such as mackerel would eat a smaller quantity of fish to meet a particular energy need than one which selected cod, which has a much lower calorie content. The estimated annual energy budget of Grey Seals suggests that the average daily intake is about 5 kg (11 pounds) of fish per day. However, individuals probably do not feed every day and they fast during the breeding season, females for at least three weeks and males for up to six weeks.

The feeding of seals is a subject which has been much discussed and hotly debated, because seals are frequently regarded as competitors with man for fish stocks. The ways in which man and seals interact are discussed in a later chapter.

Reproduction

PUPPING

Sleek fat pregnant females begin to assemble at traditional breeding sites in the late summer. They appear to spend much of their time loafing on the hauling-out sites. Most are in good condition after feeding actively for the summer months. Close to the time of birth they come ashore to the pupping grounds, as though prospecting for a suitable site. The timing varies from place to place; breeding begins in early September in south-west England and South Wales, in late September and early October in west Scotland, but it is as late as November before the first pups are born at the east coast sites of the Isle of May and the Farne Islands. The preliminary visit, which appears to be a form of reconnaissance, occurs as much as a week or as little as a day in advance of the birth. Staying ashore continuously begins about a day ahead of birth. Labour is not an obvious process in seals; females may become restless, constantly changing position and perhaps scratching at the ground with a fore-flipper. Occasionally the flanks may be seen to heave, presumably as contractions occur. But birth itself is rapid and the first sign that a pup has arrived is often the wheeling and squabbling of gulls over the membranes which enclosed the pup.

Immediately after the birth the female turns to the white-coated pup and sniffs it, touching it with her nose. She will do this several times in the first half hour after birth, learning its smell. The pup is a skinny 13-14 kg (29-31 pounds) when born, with folds of skin wrinkling its neck and body. Its movements are badly co-ordinated on land, and if it inadvertently entered the water at this stage, it would have problems with the cold. The female attends her pup closely, reacting aggressively to other seals which come close and to the gulls which gather to fight over the membranes and the placenta which is expelled about ten minutes after birth.

The pup may attempt to suck within a few minutes of birth, and all normal pups will have fed within six hours. First attempts are usually fumbling efforts on the part of both mother and pup. The female heels over on her side as the pup nuzzles her, searching for the nipples, which are set towards the tail end of the belly. As part of the seal's streamlining the nipples are usually inverted but the pup's nosing in their vicinity causes them to pop out. To help the pup locate the right area, the female may push it gently down her body using a characteristic up and down movement of her fore-flipper, known as flippering. Once contact is made the pup latches on, wrapping the indented tip of its tongue around the nipple. It then sucks for several minutes before changing to the other nipple. The end of the bout is usually indicated by pup switching frequently between the mammary glands. The duration of suckling bouts varies considerably between mother-pup pairs, but the average duration is just under ten minutes, and there are about five or six such bouts each day. The growth rate of pups is slow for the first day or so while the pup's ability to suck improves and the mother's milk flow is established, but soon the pup is profi-

17. *Early lactation, fat mother, thin pup.*

cient at locating the nipples and it increases in size at a phenomenal rate on its diet of fat-rich milk. Grey Seal milk contains up to 60 per cent fat and is more like mayonnaise in consistency than milk. Pup weight doubles in just over one week, increasing daily by almost 2 kg (4½ pounds). At the end of the lactation period lasting sixteen to eighteen days pups will have trebled their birth weight, becoming chubby barrels weighing about 45 kg (100 pounds). They do not grow much in length over this time but increase their girth, accumulating a thick layer of blubber under their skin which will act as an insulator as well as a food store in the weeks to come.

Mothers, however, become much thinner, losing their former rotund shape.

They do not feed while they are suckling their young but supply their own metabolic and activity costs as well as the immense energetic drain of rich milk production from stored fat. Females lose about 4 kg (9 pounds) in weight every day while ashore with their young. In energy terms this is equivalent to about seventy cream buns per day. The initial weight of around 170 kg (3½ cwt) is reduced by 65 kg (145 pounds). The fat sleek seals become serpent-like creatures with protruding hip bones. Towards the end of lactation females come into oestrus and are mated by one or more of the males in the breeding group. They then leave the breeding sites, abandoning pups to their own devices. At about three weeks of age the pups lose their white natal fur,

18. *Late lactation, thin mother, fat pup.*

19. *Two males exchange threats.*

revealing the sleek dark or silvery coat of adulthood.

MATING

What have the males been doing while females are engaged in the energetically extravagant process of lactation? The males come ashore when the first pups are born and compete with each other for a position in the breeding group. Like females, they do not feed during the breeding season, but live off their stored fat. They lose weight at the rate of 2.2 kg (5 pounds) per day, considerably less than that of lactating females. Grey Seals are polygynous — that is, some males successfully exclude others so that the sex ratio is skewed. There may be as few as two or as many as ten females to each male. It was once thought that the males held territories which they defended and into which females came to give birth. But observations now suggest that it is the females which determine the distribu-

20. *Nuptial bliss.*

tion of animals ashore by selecting where they will give birth. The males take up positions within the groups of females and then defend their right to stay in the group. Relationships between these dominant males are relatively amicable. They will exchange threats when the distance between them gets too small, but the most active encounters are usually between them and non-established males which are trying to get close to females. However, when two giants do fight, the battle can be spectacular with the exchange of savage bites, leaving their necks streaming with blood.

How dominance relationships between males are established is not yet known in detail. We do know that although males are sexually mature at the age of six they do not gain a place within the breeding group until they are ten. Size and mating success are correlated; successful males which gain a place ashore range in size from 200 to 350 kg (4 to 7 cwt), and, of these, the largest males may mate with ten times more females than their smallest rivals. Although size is an advantage in combat, the more important aspect for a Grey Seal male may be the ability to stay ashore for a long period of time. Large animals have proportionally larger energy stores than smaller ones. By staying ashore for several weeks, even while fasting, males can overlap in time with many females, which remain on shore only for the eighteen or so days of lactation. In this way males can increase their chances of siring more offspring. Their attention is directed solely towards that aim — they take no part in parental care.

The cues which signal that a female is receptive may not be very specific, because males often attempt to mount females which are in an early stage of lactation. Females tend to react aggressively to the approach of a male, even when they are in oestrus and the end result may be a copulation. There is the possibility that the female's aggression may incite male competition, which may enhance the female's opportunities for mate choice. Copulations last on average for twenty minutes and each female may be mated up to three times, not necessarily by the same male.

DEVELOPMENT OF THE EMBRYO

Soon after mating the female leaves the land, abandoning the pup ashore. The fertilised egg inside the uterus divides about four times and then stops. Development is suspended for around four months until the time of the moult, when implantation occurs. The egg then becomes attached to the uterine wall, a placenta forms and normal development continues for seven months. Suspended development, or delayed implantation, is a mechanism in Grey Seals for ensuring synchrony of pupping when gestation occupies less than a year. This must be particularly important to a species which spends most of its year dispersed at sea.

Life and death

There is a considerable disparity between the lifespans of male and female Grey Seals. The oldest female ever recorded was a 46-year-old from Shetland, but few live more than 35 years. The oldest male was a Canadian specimen of 29 years, but not many survive beyond the age of 25. Females reach sexual maturity between the ages of three and five, so their reproductive life may go on for more than 25 years. But they do not have a pup every year; the information we have suggests that on average they fail to become pregnant once every ten years. Males reach sexual maturity when they are six but do not usually gain and hold a position in a breeding group until they are nearer ten. We do not yet know how successful Grey Seal males are at breeding every year once they are sexually and socially mature. Studies on Elephant Seals indicate that individual males dominate the breeding scene for one or at most two years, even though they may be present for several consecutive seasons.

How do we know how old seals are? When they are alive it is very difficult to age them, apart from saying, for instance, that one individual looks grizzled and therefore must be old, or another has few scars and unworn teeth and looks young.

But when seals die they can be aged accurately from annual growth rings laid down in their teeth or in the cementum. These are 'read' by cutting a thin section of one of the canines, the biggest teeth, and examining the section under a microscope. Alternating light and dark bands, which must be caused by changes in the seal's annual activities, such as fasting during the breeding season, can then be counted. Experts can detect changes in the width of bands which occur in the teeth of females when they first begin to have pups. So the age of first breeding can be determined in these animals.

Not all Grey Seals survive to reach a ripe old age. Like most animals, Grey Seals suffer a high mortality in the early stages of their life. 5 per cent are lost as still births and a large number of pups do not survive the short but intense process of lactation. The mortality on beaches is usually between 15 and 25 per cent, but at some localities it may be as high as 40 per cent. Crowded sites or wave-swept beaches are most likely to have large numbers of dead pups. The process of learning to feed for themselves must also result in many casualties. Overall, about two-thirds of pups born reach their first birthday. After that, their chances of survival are higher: about 93 per cent survive each year from then onwards except for breeding males, which have an 80 per cent annual survival rate.

The primary causes of death in pups are starvation, usually as a result of the failure of the bond between mother and pup, and infections by various pathogens. The causes of adult mortality have not yet been quantified, but pleurisy, pneumonia and mucous congestion of the lungs have been identified as important disorders. Grey Seals have few predators in the oceans. Killer Whales may attack seals occasionally and off the Canadian coast Great White Sharks may take weaned pups as they leave the breeding sites. But on land the Grey Seal's major predator, man, can have a devastating effect on numbers.

Grey Seals and man

EXPLOITATION AND CONSERVATION

Seals are an attractive prey item to hunters. They are large and thus offer a good return for the time spent in pursuit. To the terrestrial predator they are an easy target ashore because their adaptations to aquatic living make them clumsy on land. Their thick layers of blubber and fur coats are valuable resources, in addition to the meat they can provide. Coast-dwelling man has had a long association with seals, as indicated by the abundant remains in the middens of ancient settlements, such as Jarlshof in Shetland. Grey Seals have been hunted throughout their range, resulting perhaps in numbers being kept in check. During the nineteenth century subsistence hunting was replaced by commercial hunting of pups for skins. In Britain in 1914 it was suggested that the Grey Seal population was as low as five hundred individuals. This suggestion led to the Grey Seal Protection Act of 1914, which provided a close season. The legislation was reformulated in 1932, and the current act, the Conservation of Seals Act, which extended protection to the Common Seal for the first time, was passed in 1970. This law provides protection during the breeding seasons but also permits licences to be issued for the taking of seals for various purposes, such as commercial exploitation or fisheries protection. Canada and most European countries which have Grey Seals have passed laws which either protect the species or control its hunting. Under international laws there is a ban on the import of seal skins by those countries which signed the Gdansk Convention, and the Grey Seal is being added to the schedule of protected migratory species under the Bonn Convention.

CHANGES IN NUMBERS

While the 1914 estimate of five hundred Grey Seals in Britain was probably too low, there is no doubt that in the

21. Hunters gather piles of blood-stained skins of Grey Seal pups.

second half of the twentieth century there has been a marked increase in numbers. The best documented increase is at the Farne Islands in Northumberland. These islands were designated in 1925 as a reserve for the variety of wildlife which frequented the site, in particular sea-birds, but including about a hundred Grey Seals which bred there. The owners of the islands, the National Trust, expressed concern in the early 1970s that there were then over two thousand pups born and that the seals were causing damage to the thin soil cap on some of the islands. Since then, seals have been encouraged to breed on the rocky islands, which are less susceptible to soil damage, and numbers have been reduced.

Elsewhere in Britain a similar increase in Grey Seal numbers has occurred, although information is less precise than at the Farnes because the population estimates for the first half of the twentieth century were rather poor. The first systematic studies of Grey Seals in Scotland were made in the 1960s, and, as a result of continuous improvement in survey techniques and estimation methods, Grey Seals in Britain are perhaps one of the best known large mammal populations in the world. In 1966 the United Kingdom population of Grey Seals was estimated at 34,200 and the world total at 52,500. The 1987 estimates were about 100,000 for the United Kingdom and between 200,000 and 250,000 for the world population.

What are the causes of this increase? Protective legislation has undoubtedly played a major part but changes in human demography are also thought to have had an effect. During the nineteenth century many of the outer islands of Britain, in particular the Hebrides, were deserted by their human inhabitants. This depopulation not only decreased hunting pressure on seals but also increased the availability of breeding habitat. While we cannot be sure that Grey Seals were limited in the past by space for breeding, there is no doubt that they were quick to colonise newly available sites. The best example of this is the Monach isles in the Outer Hebrides. These beautiful, low-lying, shell-sand islands were deserted by their human residents in 1949. A small number of seals bred there in the early 1960s; by 1985 the islands were producing over four thousand pups annually, making it one of the largest Grey Seal breeding sites in the world.

A more recent factor which has influenced hunting pressure on seals has been a marked change in public attitudes towards killing animals for their skins. Some conservation bodies have waged successful campaigns against the wearing of furs in many European countries which used to be the main markets for fur products. The Council of the European Communities has banned the import of skins of some species of seals, and there is strong opposition to fur fashion amongst the general public. With no demand for the products, the value of skins has declined and consequently requests for licences to hunt seals commercially in Britain and elsewhere in Europe have largely ceased.

While hunting may no longer pose a problem for seals, they do not have an untroubled relationship with humans. Seals eat fish, and many fishermen see them as competitors for the resources of the sea.

SEALS AND FISHERIES

The increase in Grey Seal numbers which began in the first half of the twentieth century set off complaints during the 1950s about the impact which seals were having on fisheries. The first problems arose with the salmon net fisheries which occur predominantly on the east coast of Scotland and northern England. These fisheries put out nets of various designs at fixed places along the coast. The nets act as traps into which salmon and sea trout swim as they move along the coast or in and out of the rivers. Seals can be serious pests at these nets at various times of the year. Common Seals were often the culprits when damage levels before the 1950s were low but they were superseded by Grey Seals, which soon became the salmon netsmen's principal enemy. They enter nets to take fish but do not restrict themselves to one: they may damage the whole catch by taking bites out of all the fish. Alternatively they may bite and claw at fish through the mesh without entering the net. Before the 1960s seals caused damage to the nets themselves, which were then made of natural fibres, but the introduction of man-made fibres has greatly reduced that problem.

The salmon-netting industry has kept records of seal damage to its fisheries for several decades; information has been gathered both on attacks at nets and on the incidence of damaged fish received at the markets. From these records it has been found that some sites are much more afflicted by seal damage than others and that levels vary seasonally. In Scotland the highest levels occur in the spring, when salmon catches are at their lowest. Levels of damage are apparently unrelated to absolute numbers of seals, because damage at east coast Scottish sites has not increased since the early 1960s, while the Grey Seal population has more than doubled. Seals are also thought to attack fish away from the nets, as fish with partially healed claw marks often appear in the catches. Up to 6 per cent of the salmon catch may show signs of either recent or healed seal attack.

Why cannot attempts be made to protect nets? Many different solutions have been tried but most are ineffective or uneconomic. The entrances to nets were reduced in size to prevent seals from getting in but that had a tendency to discourage fish from entering too, which defeated the object of the exercise. Poisoning raiders with strychnine-baited fish was said to be effective, but its use is now banned under the Conservation of Seals Act. Playing sounds to scare seals was tried, but the initial success soon wore off, and it could be that in time the seals might learn to regard the sounds as an invitation to take the fish. There are frequent calls for seal culls to reduce numbers generally, but as the evidence points to a weak relationship between numbers and damage an unacceptably drastic reduction would probably be needed before any change might be detected. Shooting offending seals seems to be the only effective measure, although that can present problems if the net is near to inhabited parts of the shore or the marksman has to operate from a bobbing boat.

A new type of fishery has come to the

fore since the mid 1970s and is at the centre of a growth industry in Scotland. Salmon and sea trout are reared in net cages moored in sheltered inlets. It did not take seals long to discover these cages. Sheltered waters are favoured by Common Seals, so they have been more of a problem than Grey Seals at these nets. The incidence and severity of damage varies from site to site, but most cages currently in use can be effectively protected by a screen of anti-predator nets.

An increase in Grey Seal numbers has been associated with a rising level of infestation of a parasitic nematode worm in fish of the cod family. Grey Seals are hosts to the codworm *(Pseudoterranova decipiens)*, which passes its final larval stage in the fish. Although it is killed by freezing or cooking, codworm detracts from the attractiveness of a fish fillet to the would-be consumer, so the marketability of the fish is reduced, or the costs of handling go up as the worms have to be removed by hand. However, although the incidence of codworm in fish did increase during the 1950s and early 1960s, it then levelled off while seal numbers continued to increase. The incidence of infestation requires the presence of seals, but levels are not obviously related to the number of seals. Severe problems have been reported from some areas, such as some localities on the Norwegian coast, and there has been a marked increase in codworm infestation in Canada, coinciding with a rise in Grey Seal numbers there. Thus, while in Britain it seems that reducing seal numbers would not affect worm burdens in fish, the evidence from Canada points to a possible link between seal numbers and infestation.

Another area of conflict which has resulted in calls for a reduction in seal numbers is that of general competition for fish stocks between seals and people. It is argued that seals eat large quantities of commercially valuable species of fish, which are therefore not available to be caught, and the result is a net loss to the fishery. Various attempts have been made since the 1960s by the fisheries departments to reduce seal numbers, mainly by killing large numbers of pups. Culls took place in Orkney in 1962, followed by the setting of an annual pup quota, and at the Farne Islands in 1963-5. The most recent proposal for a major cull of Grey Seals came in 1976, when it was estimated that Grey Seal predation cost the industry £15-20 million annually, a calculation based on the assumption that half of the seal's catch would be available if the population was wiped out. It was suggested that numbers should be reduced to the level of the early 1960s, when there were apparently far fewer incidents of damage to fisheries. A combination of adult and pup culls over a period of several years, starting in 1977, was proposed to achieve this aim, but the plan was abandoned after two years. Strong protests by the public and by the environmental lobby that there was insufficient evidence to prove the case against the Grey Seal caused the Department of Agriculture and Fisheries for Scotland (DAFS) to reconsider the problem.

A major research programme on the interactions between seals and fisheries was funded by DAFS between 1980 and 1984. The studies were carried out by the Sea Mammal Research Unit of the Natural Environment Research Council and covered many facets of the problem. It explored the nature and extent of damage to salmon fisheries, using both old records and new observations. Grey Seal diet was studied using faecal analysis, and food requirements were determined through energy studies. Advances were made in studying the distribution of seals at sea by telemetry. The results of these various approaches were drawn together in mathematical models. Although the work confirmed the incidence of damage at salmon nets, it demonstrated the lack of relationship between levels of damage and absolute seal numbers. Diet was shown to vary seasonally and with locality, but in all areas sand-eels were important food items for the seals. It was concluded that a general reduction in seal numbers would be unlikely to have a direct effect on commercial fish catches.

However, the conclusions reached in this study were unpopular with the fishing bodies. Calls for culls are being renewed and DAFS is funding its own seal studies. At present (1987), no pups are hunted and the only seals killed are in the vicinity of nets or for specific cases of habitat protection. The debates on the significance of seal predation will no doubt continue for many years to come, but at least the continuing advances in our understanding of seals and how they interact with their environment mean that the debates should be better informed, even if it is a long time before we have an adequate understanding of the complex interactions of biological systems.

POLLUTION

In their position at the ends of marine food chains, Grey Seals have often been regarded as potential sumps for pollutants affecting the marine environment. Studies have concentrated on heavy metals and organochlorine compounds, mainly DDT, dieldrin and PCBs. High levels of mercury have been discovered in livers of Grey Seals both in east Scotland and Canada, but most of this is in a non-toxic, inorganic form. Only about 5 per cent of the mercury is present as methyl mercury, and even that may not be a problem to seals because there is some evidence to suggest that they can de-methylate it. Mercury may accumulate with age in seals, so that high levels are not necessarily a reflection of severe environmental contamination. There is enormous variation in the burdens of organochlorine compounds carried by different animals. Some very high levels have been found in a few seals from British coasts, but in general the highest concentrations are in Grey Seals from the Baltic. The population there is giving serious cause for concern; it is declining mainly though reproductive failure and there is a high incidence of disorders such as hair loss, skull deformities and gut ulcerations, all of which may be associated with a high intake of organochlorine compounds in the fish diet. A study of Common Seals has shown a link between PCB levels in diet and poor breeding success in females, which probably operates through disturbance to the hormones which control implantation of embryos.

Because of the devastating effect that oil has on seabirds, it was first thought that seals might also suffer problems from it. But because they do not groom their fur and do not rely on it as much as their fat for maintaining their body temperature, the effects of oil are rarely deleterious for Grey Seals. They can suffer irritated eyes from oil, but that soon improves if they move away from the polluted area. There are some reports of young animals dying as a result of swallowing oil.

A less obvious but more insidious contaminant is radioactivity. So much attention is given to nuclear power stations and processing plants, which are an important source of marine radioactivity, that it might be thought that seals would be well studied. However, much of the research in this field has been directed towards contamination of organisms which might end up as food for man. As Grey Seals are not eaten by humans in Britain, their contamination levels are unknown. Following the Chernobyl nuclear accident in 1986, and with the increased public concern about low-level discharges from nuclear installations, research in this field is just beginning.

How and where to see Grey Seals

Several zoos and marine life centres hold Grey Seals, for instance Edinburgh Zoo and the Seal Sanctuary at Helston in Cornwall. There individuals can be seen at close quarters, but it is not the same as seeing them in the wild. Marine mammals are not the easiest of beasts for land-bound people to study. For a large part of the year Grey Seals are dispersed at sea, but they do haul out between feeding forays, sometimes on skerries quite close to the mainland. In the summer local boatmen in the right localities can run a brisk trade in ferrying visitors out to see the seals. Examples of sites where Grey Seals can be seen are the Farne Islands, Northumberland, and Ramsey and Skomer islands near St Davids, Dyfed. These conducted tours are probably the best way of getting to see large numbers of seals.

A casual observer is unlikely to find access to breeding sites easy. Grey Seals choose remote coasts and islands which are difficult to get to in the stormy weather which is so frequent in the autumn. In Canada and the Baltic many animals breed on the floating pack ice in the late winter or early spring. In Britain many of the breeding islands are nature reserves, so permits may be needed to visit them. Human visitors are not encouraged by those responsible for Grey Seal breeding localities because of the disturbance people cause, not necessarily intentionally, but merely by their presence. Adult seals may stampede into the sea, perhaps squashing pups in their panic. Touching seal pups is not advisable, however appealing the soft-eyed creatures seem, because they have a set of extremely sharp teeth. Indeed, a licence is needed under the Conservation of Seals Act to handle seals during the close season, unless the person is attempting to help a sick animal. Most people who go to enough trouble to visit a Grey Seal breeding site are likely to have a specific objective in mind, such as photography, and will avoid causing disturbance as far as possible. Visitors should remember that vision is not the only sense that seals use to detect potential enemies — they have a very keen sense of smell. Ducking behind a rock will not prevent an observer from being noticed if he or she is upwind, and lighting a cigarette can cause a mass exit.

Encountering large numbers of seals is therefore likely to require a boat trip and a lot of organisation. There are many places on the coast, however, where a Grey Seal may appear. There are said to be resident seals in some of the fishing harbours, such as Stornoway, Western Isles, and Ullapool, Highland, which grow fat on offerings from the fishing boats. The probability of casual sightings is more likely near large concentrations of seals, but it is impossible to be certain of seeing a seal at any particular place. Part of the pleasure of spotting one is the unexpectedness of a solemn, whiskery face staring from out of the waves.

If a lone white-coated pup is found on a beach, it should not be assumed that it is abandoned and in trouble unless it is very obviously injured or starving. An anxious female seal may be waiting offshore for the intruder to depart, or the pup may already be weaned and ready for independent life. It is best to retire to a distance and observe the animal. If it is healthy it will probably depart in its own chosen time, but if it remains there for many hours and appears to have problems, then call for advice from an organisation such as the RSPCA. It should not be taken home: hand-rearing seals so that they can eventually be released into the wild is a special skill.

Further reading

Hewer, H. R. *British Seals*. Collins New Naturalist, 1974. (Now rather out of date.)
King, Judith. *Seals of the World*. British Museum (Natural History). Oxford University Press, 1984. (An excellent general account of all species of seals.)

Much of the published scientific work on Grey Seals has been carried out by the Sea Mammal Research Unit, which is part of the Natural Environment Research Council. A full list of publications is available from SMRU, c/o British Antarctic Survey, High Cross, Madingley Road, Cambridge CB3 0ET.

·ACKNOWLEDGEMENTS

Thanks to my husband, Peter, for tea, sympathy and for reading the manuscript, to Rowena Baker and Mike Fedak, who made helpful comments on the first draft, to Chris Gilbert, who kindly assisted with the preparation of photographs, and to Jan Parr, who took so much trouble in preparing the drawings.

Illustrations are acknowledged to: Ian Boyd, 18; Jan Parr, 2, 5, 6 and 16; Sea Mammal Research Unit, 3, 8, 9 and 17. All other illustrations are by the author.